Tween Time

Over 52 Ways to Celebrate Life With Kids Ages 8-12

Ginny Bishop

with Kim Griffeth

Illustrated By Camille Solarte

Text copyright © 2003 by Ginny Bishop
Illustrations copyright © 2003 by Camille Solarte

All rights reserved. No part of this book may be reproduced by any means whatsoever, either mechanical or electronic, without written permission from the publisher, except for brief passages quoted for purposes of review.

Note: Some activities suggested in this book require help and supervision from adults. The publisher and authors assume no responsibility for any damages or injuries incurred by performing any of the activities in this book.

Cover illustration and interior illustrations by Camille Solarte
Cover and interior design, design consultation by Montezon Design
Edited by Maureen Cotter
Logotype design by Leibson McGrath, Inc.
Cover photo by Holley Huggins
Back cover photo by Roy Willey

ISBN #9 780972 120104 51095

Happy Life Press
P.O. Box 270556
Littleton, CO 80127

E-mail: HappyLifePress@aol.com
Website: www.TweenTime.com

Printed in the United States of America

Love to my seven shooting stars.
You're my very own constellation.

—Ginny

To Jenn, Jess and Garrett,
my three wishing stars.

—Kim

TWEEN TIME

CONTENTS

Dear Friends of Tweens 1

What It's All About 3

I'll Promise You, You Promise Me 11

Where Are We Going? 13

Develop a New View 15

Get Your Rake and Go 17

Take Me Out to the Ballgame 19

007 21

It's All About Me 23

Cindy Crawford, Move Over! 25

What Mothers Do Best 27

Boogie Down! 29

When I Was Little 31

The One That Got Away 33

Hike by the Light of the Moon 35

Be Tightwads Together 37

Calling All Music Lovers 39

32-53-15 41

Tell Me Something New 43

Be the King or Queen of Your Castle 45

You Be Me, I'll Be You 47

Watch Me Grow 49

Tie One On 51

Be Grateful 53

Strike or Spare? 55

Ham It Up! 57

Jam Session 101 59

What's it Worth? 61

Do Ya Care? 63

Sew What? 65

Let Freedom Ring 67

Find the Best of Everything 69

Go. Fight. Win! 71

Om 73

Chief Cook and Bottle Washer 75

Ready? Set. Surprise! 77

Feng Shui, A Tween's Way 79

Be Bookworms Together 81

Fourth Down. A Yard To Go. 83

4 Green Thumbs Are Better Than 2 85

Bon Appetit! 87

Calling All Artists 89

Some Like It Hot! 91

Butcher, Baker, Candlestick Maker 93

Just the Two of Us 95

Box Your Stress Away 97

Here's What I Do Know 99

Pump It Up! 101

You Be Black, I'll Be Red 103

Happy Birthday to Us 105

Massage, Anyone? 107

Be Vincent Van Gogh 109

Share Your Favorite Books 110

Twinkle, Twinkle, My Little Star 113

So Now What? 115

The Big Thanks 117

All About Us 118

Dear Friends of Tweens,

Are you looking for some creative ways to have fun with that special tween in your life?

Well, here you go: Over 52 fabulous ways to reconnect with that terrific kid. You know, that kid who isn't begging to go to the playground with you anymore, but isn't driving himself to soccer just yet. These kids are somewhere from 8 to 12 years old, and they need you, probably more than they might admit. They need you to make a promise to be there, to spend time having fun with them and learning about them.

My friend Kim and I dreamed up *Tween Time* one afternoon when the lemonade was cold and the ideas were hot. We were wishing that we could freeze time. Freeze it at that moment when we were friendly and comfortable with our kids and their friends and didn't have to try to reinvent time together. And that's how it all started.

We wrote *Tween Time* in the car-pool line and e-mailed each other changes in the middle of the night and by cell phone during soccer tournaments and piano recitals. My tween-age daughter, Camille, doodled her way onto the pages of the book with her whimsical illustrations.

Tween Time is our first symphony, written to give parents, grandparents, godparents, aunts, uncles and friends new ways to connect with that great kid in their lives. These aren't ideas that we overheard at some cocktail party or read about in the newspaper. *Tween Time* is our real lives, written down.

We're proud to say that *Tween Time* is a selection of activities we've done—and still do—with our tweens and their friends. I'm still listening to my oldest son's first rock band; I've hosted the "Bishop-Solarte Spa" more than once in our bathroom, and we make a point to update our family grateful journal almost every day. Kim has the pictures to show the forts she has built with her tweens, and she and her daughters regularly stage impromtu fashion shows in their living room, showing off new outfits. We are real-life moms doing real-life stuff with our tweens. Maybe they're not big ideas, but they are big fun.

Whether you're an aunt or a stepparent, a mentor to tweens in your church or school group, or even if you're a busy parent raising your own tween, *Tween Time* is for you.

Get inspired. These are open-ended, magical journeys that tend to take on lives of their own. It's all about forming an alliance. Making a promise and keeping it. Doing real-life stuff that makes you happy, together.

So read on. Pick an adventure. Make it happen. Laugh. Pray. Talk. Listen. Be curious. With your favorite tween.

Have fun!

Ginny

WHAT IT'S ALL ABOUT

James Vollbracht writes in his highly acclaimed book, *Stopping At Every Lemonade Stand*, ". . . when I **ASK KIDS** what the number one thing they want from adults is, the answer is always time. And, more time. . . . Our kids need adults who know how to do things with them, and not to them."

Tween Time is a "**HOW-TO**" resource guide that gets you out of your routine and into spending time doing fun things with that terrific tween in your life. These are creative ideas that really work. We know they work because we've tried them!

"**LET'S DO THIS TOGETHER** sometime, alone," my son, Dylan, suggested after our family took a spontaneous bus tour of our city.

"Now that was really fun," Kim's daughter, Jess, said after a night of family storytelling.

And that's what our kids continue to tell us: that one-on-one time, doing just about anything that's fun, **MAKES THEM FEEL SPECIAL**. And that's what this book is all about.

So find an adventure here that will help you connect with your tween. Laugh out loud if it tickles your funny bone. Cry if it brings back memories of your own childhood. Better yet, read what our tweens have to say about each one.

They'll give you **THE REAL SKINNY**.

"Whoa! **WAIT A MINUTE!**" you find yourself saying. "There aren't enough hours in the day!"

We know it's hard. We're not Super Moms. I have a part-time job and parent six kids with my husband, and Kim, a single mom, works two jobs and has three kids. **WE'RE CHALLENGED BY THE SAME**

DAILY TASKS you face: doing laundry, meeting deadlines at work, car-pooling, supervising homework and making dinner. We have rough times with our kids and our lives, just as you do.

But Kim and I found that time alone with our favorite tweens makes everything better. So we've learned to **CARVE OUT THE TIME.** Kim makes sure she sits at the dinner table when her tweens are planning to feng shui their bedrooms on a shoestring budget. I make sure I write my tween's secret pen pal letter after she's gone to bed. What we've learned from having kids is that you must take some time—monthly, weekly, daily—to reconnect with that special tween in your life.

WE'LL SHOW YOU HOW.

Tween Time includes a wide selection of adventures to capture the

interest of every tween: **BOYS AND GIRLS;** kids of all colors; in every zip code; artists and athletes. There's something in this book for everyone. So make a promise to do some real-life stuff that makes you happy, together. Just get going!

And do it before that tween becomes a teenager. Because, in a lot of ways, this is your last chance before the turmoil of adolescence. As Laura Sessions Stepp writes in *Our Last Best Shot*, "The early adolescent years are not only our **LAST BEST SHOT** at guiding our children, they're our last best shot at being guided by our children before we lose them to the world."

DON'T SWEAT IT if you don't try every adventure in this book. Even if you make just one journey, you're on your way.

We would love to hear your story. You can reach us at:

WWW.TWEENTIME.COM

I like when my Mom plans something alone with me because it makes me feel like I'm not just another somebody.

Dylan, 11

I'LL PROMISE YOU, YOU PROMISE ME

Make this book a keepsake of your adventures with your tween.

But don't make it a big scrapbook project. Just slap some pictures of the two of you in between the pages. Stuff the hockey ticket stubs and the receipt from the local diner in here, too.

If you have something to say after a good time together, jot it down in the margin. It doesn't have to be fancy.

It's just a reminder for another day. A reminder that the two of you can have fun together.

Make it a diving board for your relationship. Let it launch something new and more wonderful than you might have imagined.

Find something you like to do and take a friend—a tween. Make a pact. Form an alliance. Fulfill a dream. Laugh together. Share a fear.

And make a promise: Promise to meet halfway. Be curious with a tween and develop a real connection that will last.

Good luck. Have fun!

The best part about bus trippin' is you're so surprised.

Jenn, 13

WHERE ARE WE GOING?

Go bus trippin' with your tween.

Take a spontaneous and crazy journey. Load your tween on the city bus. Let him think he's going to run errands with you. Allow him to groan a few times at the thought of a day with you—on the bus.

Then give him a bag of clues to see if he can guess what's going on. It doesn't have to cost anything. Throw in a toy pail and shovel for a clue about a trip to the beach or make a copy of a city map and lead him on a wild-goose chase on paper. Think of it as a scavenger hunt in which you're both trying to find each other.

It can be just a detour for the day to an old-fashioned burger joint or a trip to a historic spot in your hometown. You decide.

Wherever you go, make it funny. Trick him with misleading clues. And don't make it too easy. Tweens love to be stumped.

Maybe it's a sleepover at the natural history museum, or a day building sand castles on the beach—make it a sweet surprise for your tween.

DEVELOP A NEW VIEW

Go on a photo shoot with your favorite tween. You can use two cameras—cheap, disposable cameras will do. Stick with color or shoot black and white for a change. Experiment with light and your smiling faces. Don't limit yourself to just outdoor scenes. Find some interesting indoor lighting opportunities in your town and be creative.

Chronicle your day's shoot in a small photo album dedicated to you and your tween. If still photography isn't your gig, make a movie with your video camera. You don't have to be an award-winning photojournalist to have fun with photography.

Revisit this keepsake once a year, share memories and marvel at how fast your tween is growing.

I like to help the old man on our street rake the leaves. It makes our leaf pile bigger!

Garrett, 10

GET YOUR RAKE AND GO

Is there someone in your neighborhood who would love to have some help with yard work? Maybe it's an elderly neighbor, a family with newborn twins or a single mom.

Just look around and ring a doorbell. Offer to mow the lawn, rake the leaves, pull some stubborn weeds, plant and tend a vegetable garden, plant some flower boxes or take the trash bins out on trash day.

Do it once a month or more often. It means a lot to neighbors in need, and your tween will see your warm heart in action.

Going to see a ballgame in the cheap seats is awesome because you don't have to be quiet.

Kiefer, 8

TAKE ME OUT TO THE BALLGAME

There's nothing like the smell of hot, roasted peanuts, the crack of the bat and the taste of a steamed hot dog on a warm summer night. How about introducing your tween to the sights and sounds of that great American pastime, baseball.

You say you can't afford high-priced tickets for a Bruins, Rockies or Cubs game? Think again. In every ballpark, there is a bleacher or Rockpile section with seats that cost next to nothing. Call your local stadium to find out about bargains and ask about special kids' promotions. Some teams even let kids run the bases. In some towns, there's also a minor-league baseball team or farm club, where you can get all the flavor of the game in a cozy stadium for a lot less.

It's more fun in the cheap seats—where the sodas are just as cold, and the cheers are deafening. And don't forget—here's a chance to make a fool of yourself: Sing "Take Me Out To The Ballgame" a hundred times, make up a goofy dance that wins you the honor of an appearance on the scoreboard monitor, and dream about catching a fly ball in your very own glove.

At the end of the game, you probably won't even care whether your team won the game.

My friends think I'm lucky

because my Mom fills my suitcase

with funny love notes.

Jess, 12

007

Be a secret pen pal.

Try to stump the master. Write a letter on your word processor or typewriter so he won't recognize your handwriting. Mail it from an unfamiliar zip code. Just give him a smattering of clues about the author. Share things about your life. Let him know what matters, what hurts, what scares you and what makes you happy.

Don't slip it under his pillow. Don't e-mail it. Do it the old-fashioned way: Stamp it and mail it. Let him see that someone took the time to send REAL mail.

See how long it takes him to figure out your identity.

IT'S ALL ABOUT ME

Everyone is great at saving that lock of hair from Baby's first haircut and writing down her first words, steps and other milestones in a beautiful baby book. But what about creating a book that's about your tween's life?

Why not surprise her with a compilation of all that's neat about her today? Throw in some snapshots of her recent triumphs. Paste in a few great photos of that time you went fishing at the lake near Grandma's house. Reminisce about the cute things she has said. Write it down and tape the list to these pages.

Add some stories about your life as a tween; talk about what makes your tween different from other siblings and her peers; list ten things that make you love him like no one else.

Include some artwork or class projects that he's especially proud of, and let him add some touches of his own. Maybe you just want to design or decorate it together and compile the guts as you go along, or start the book as a gift for her and add to it.

Whatever suits your tween and your tempo. Just celebrate life with your tween.

Sometimes it's a big drama getting ready for school in the morning. If we've already had a 'fashion show,' it helps me know what goes with what.

Jenn, 13

CINDY CRAWFORD, MOVE OVER!

Make a date with your daughter and set up the runway for your own private fashion show. The runway can just be a sheet you've folded over on the ground or a big coffee table sturdy enough to stand on. Find fun clothes in your closets to mix and match, or get some duds at the 99-cents sale at a local thrift store and go to town!

Be as wacky or as traditional as you want. Wear a pair of jeans with high heels and a silk top and parade up and down the runway until your feet hurt. Pin your hair up with a rhinestone barrette and experiment with makeup. Pump up the music. Videotape your fashion show—if you can stop laughing long enough.

And remember, nobody's watching!

I like our Adventure Club because my Mom is more free. She seems more happy-go-lucky than when she's driving me to stuff.

Garrett, 10

WHAT MOTHERS DO BEST

Every dad wants his son to grow up and go fishing with him. Every father longs for the days when his infant son will be old enough to play catch in the backyard.

But what are our wishes as mothers for our sons? Make memories with your son by starting a Mother/Son Outdoor Adventure Club.

Look for some eclectic mother/son pairs who can laugh at themselves. Look for moms who have more of a relationship with their sons than just being chauffeur, laundress and cook. Then send out your invitation for nine meetings a year. We've been able to dream up some fun—and free—ideas that make hanging out with our sons tons of fun.

Each mother/son pair plans an outing. We've had mother/son football games in the park, serenaded at an old folks' home and had the boys cook dinner for *us* for a change at some of our monthly meetings.

Show your son that you can run out for a pass, learn to snowboard, watercolor on the beach and make camp under the stars.

He'll laugh about how you fell 15 times while inline skating for the first time and hold sweet memories about how he got to do something for the first time with you.

And by the way, fathers know best with their daughters, too!

When you dance,

it makes you happy.

Jess, 12

BOOGIE DOWN!

Dance to my music, and I'll dance to yours.

Pump up the volume on a Saturday afternoon and make your dining room your dance floor.

Dress up in your favorite flare jeans and platform shoes and let your tween put on his own grunge-wear. Then tune into whatever music you loved when you were a tween and reminisce.

Be sure to change into your tween's duds, too, and share in his love of rap.

Whether it's the Beatles or Britney Spears, we guarantee you'll be way cool for a day. Dance till you drop!

I like stories because it gives me pictures in my mind about what my life was like.

Camille, 10

WHEN I WAS LITTLE . . .

Think about telling stories to that special tween.

Lay out on a blanket on a summer night and sit under the stars, or curl up beside a roaring fire in the winter and tell stories.

Not made-up stories. Not stories from a book. Just real stories about you, growing up.

Recount the time you caught the most fish on the family camping trip, or all the times you ran up the hundred steps to Grandma's house, or the time you hid under the back stairs while Uncle Bob looked frantically for you.

These stories are your family's legacy, and they need to be passed on to your tween. She'll love to hear about what you were like when you were a tween and how you grew up.

It won't be long until you'll hear your tween—all grown up—telling these very stories to your grandchildren.

Remember when . . .

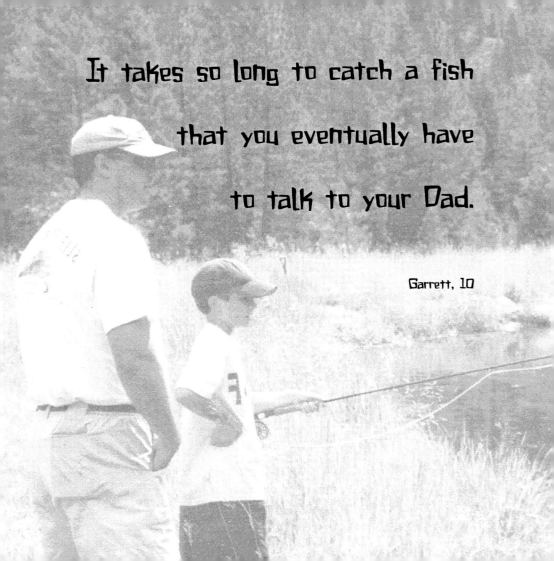

THE ONE THAT GOT AWAY

Some people like to listen to classical music in a hot bath, some like to pray with a youth group, and there are some who relax by fly-fishing.

Don't ask why fishing is a form of meditation; it just is.

Maybe it's the sound of the water lapping up against your waders or the almost silent drop of the lure into the water or the unbelievable surge of adrenaline when you get a bite.

So take your tween to the great outdoors, take a guide if you must, and learn fly-fishing. Rent the gear at a sporting goods store or just grab Grandpa's old stuff. Give it a try, you might just like it.

You might never catch a fish, but it's a good way to catch a few hours with a special tween in your life. Maybe she'll catch a new glimpse of that hip adult in her life. With this adventure, the river flows both ways.

Sometimes you'll be quiet; sometimes you'll find the silence gives way to laughter about "the one that got away."

By making memories like these, you'll be making sure your tween doesn't get away.

I like hiking by the light of the moon because there aren't any snakes around, and it is so, so very quiet that you can hear the crickets.

Kiefer, 8

HIKE BY THE LIGHT OF THE MOON

Contact your local state park to plan a guided "full moon hike" or go on your own nature hike.

Listen to the sounds of nature at night. Investigate the scat you might find at dusk. Be a nature detective and guess which animals are rustling in the underbrush.

Compare and count your sightings annually. Check out Catherine Tennant's great book, *The Box of Stars, A Practical Guide to the Night Sky and to its Myths and Legends*, from your library and study the stars.

Try to find the Big Dipper, Cassiopeia and many more. Compare winter and summer skies. Now is a good time for some interesting "Tween Talk," the sort of natural conversation that just happens when you're spending time learning and wondering at the night sky together.

Have hot chocolate and cookies, and remember.

I would hate to have to
tell kids selling cookies at
the door that we couldn't buy
any. The 'jar' makes me feel
like a good neighbor.

Jenn, 13

BE TIGHTWADS TOGETHER!

Be tightwads for two weeks and give the money you save to someone who needs it more than you do.

Fill an old mason jar with your change.

Throw in the hundreds of pennies you find under the sofa cushions, in the car or in the kitchen junk drawer. It all adds up.

Take the fifteen dollars you might have spent on a pizza and toss that in, too. Then figure out how you want to use the money. We keep the jar by the door and give some to the next kid who's selling cookies to raise money for camp.

You can support an animal shelter or use the extra cash for whatever cause you and your tween think is cool. Donate the loot in person or have it handy when the doorbell rings.

It'll make both of you feel good to share your savings.

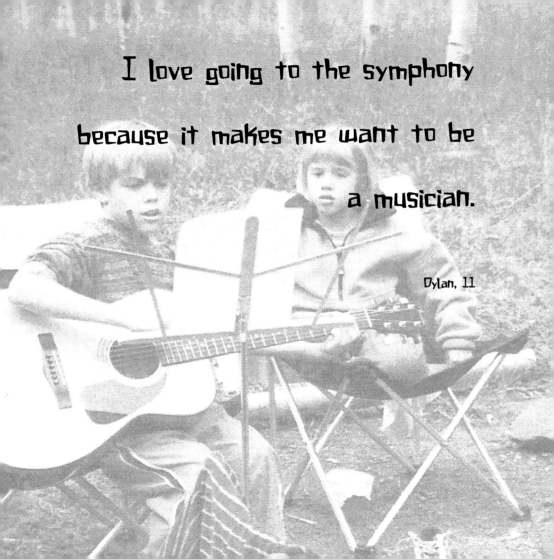

CALLING ALL MUSIC LOVERS

Get a slice of all the music your city has to offer. Take a trip to the symphony and experience classical music up close and personal. Go to a free Reggae Festival at an outdoor park and spend the day hanging and groovin' to the music. Catch a free Irish dancing festival at a local cultural center. Look for the "kids only" opera performances that charge $2 a ticket or look in the newspaper's entertainment listings to see what's free.

Celebrate your family's heritage. Go to a yodeling contest. Do the polka at a summer fair down the street.

Make a commitment to experience a different kind of music once a month for six months. It doesn't matter if it's music that you can't live without; what matters is that you can't live without time with your tween.

I loved when my Mom decorated my locker at school. It made my day to know that she loves me.

Jess, 12

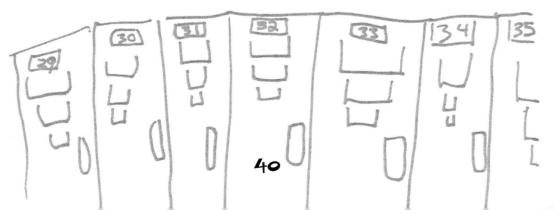

32-53-15

Here's something you can do *for* your tween. It's probably one of the few things she will let you do. Besides her laundry.

Surprise her on her own turf. Go after-hours and find your tween's school locker (remember to bring the combination) and decorate it from stem to stern. You might need to enlist the help of her best friend to make it just right.

All you need are a few rolls of tape, some photos cut with funky scissors, a bag of markers and construction paper. And voila, you have a party in a metal box.

Make it loud and unforgettable or understated and classy—whatever your tween won't hate you for doing. Believe it: Most tweens will love that you tried to honor them.

Remember to do this on the sly; tweens love surprises.

Do it to celebrate your tween's birthday, a winning soccer season or an upcoming dance performance. The occasion doesn't matter, but your tween does.

I like times like these, away
from my siblings, to learn
something new.

Camille, 10

TELL ME SOMETHING NEW

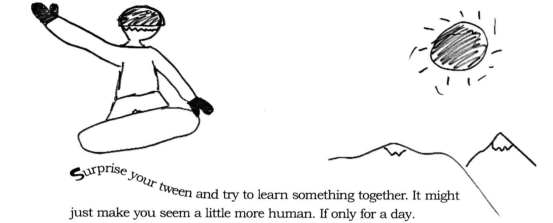

Surprise your tween and try to learn something together. It might just make you seem a little more human. If only for a day.

Maybe you've always wanted to try water-skiing—then take your tween along.

Maybe you've secretly wanted to learn how to throw pottery but didn't have a partner in crime—take your tween along.

Maybe you've always wanted to have a complete makeover at a downtown salon with your best girlfriend—take your tween along.

Just imagine how great your tween will feel when you pick him to be your pal, your co-adventurer, your friend. Just think.

Don't put a chair in the middle of your blanket fort, because you'll run into it.

Dylan, 11

BE THE KING OR QUEEN OF YOUR CASTLE

What kid hasn't wanted a tree fort for secret club meetings in her own backyard? Maybe that was your secret desire as a kid, too.

Now's the time to fulfill a dream for you *and* your tween by planning a fort-building day, weekend or month.

You can make a simple fort out of blankets and a few couches, build a snow fort after a big storm or do a full-scale, all-out fort in the backyard with scrap lumber, hammer and nails. It's up to you.

We've loved Tom Birdseye's book, *A Kid's Guide to Building Forts*, which gives the inexperienced and experienced builder alike many options.

And remember, it has little to do with the castle walls and everything to do with what goes on inside your fort. So when it's built, remember that it's not over. Crawl inside, no matter how small, and play a game of cards with your tween, read a scary ghost story or play a board game.

"Ooh" and "ah" as much as you can.

I like to give the orders sometimes. It makes me feel really important.

Kiefer, 8

YOU BE ME, I'LL BE YOU

Take the "No Whining" sign off the kitchen wall and put on a T-shirt and jeans. Let your tween dress up in your corporate best, all pressed and proper. And then switch roles for a day.

Let your tween give the orders, and you can say "No!" just the way he does. Perhaps you'll do the whining or the sulking while your tween does the yelling and the commanding.

It could be interesting to see what it's like to be on the other side. Look at yourself through the eyes of your tween and vice versa. Maybe he makes dinner that night while you make his bed and pick his clothes up off the floor. Remember: You have to try to stay in character.

Don't be nervous. Trust us, you'll laugh a lot. And next time you're giving the orders, your tone of voice might be a bit more cheerful. And who knows? Maybe your tween's tone of voice will surprise you too.

It seemed like the tree in our

front yard grew with us.

Jess, 12

WATCH ME GROW

Remember when your daughter was "Daddy's little girl" and your son was "Mommy's big guy?"

Punctuate that passage of time with a living symbol.

Plant a tree that three generations can sit under and read, have a picnic or play cards.

Go to the nursery together. Pick a tree that will thrive and add natural beauty to your landscape. And then get your shovels out and get your hands dirty.

Make your tree a meeting place, a place to take a "my tween and me" photograph every year to document how much he's grown.

When you smile for the camera, put your arm around him to steal a secret hug.

TIE ONE ON

The Christmas tree, that is.

Looking for a no-muss, no-fuss way to celebrate the holidays and to model kindness? Have a New-Age Christmas Party that even your tween will want a hand in planning.

Make the invitation list with tweens in mind. Call it "Deck the Halls with Boughs of Toothpaste" and laugh while you lick the stamps. Offer simple fare of cheese and crackers. Make a festive punch. Have your guests bring the real cheer.

Ask each guest to bring something to trim the tree. They can choose from a list of items the local shelter really needs—underwear, socks, hats and mittens. Tie the underwear and socks together to make funky garlands that will make your tree special. Use ribbon to tie toothpaste tubes and toothbrushes to each branch. Around the base of the tree, pile up toys, detergent and diapers for needy tots and their families.

Take lots of pictures. The next day, ask your tween to help you haul the loot down to the shelter. Crank up Bing Crosby and know that your tween is dreaming about the right things this Christmas.

11-15-99

Our grateful journal makes me laugh and saves my memories.

D: That the babies are finally going to come and that Taylon came out baby.

e: That the babies are going to come at 5:30 + No mo came Jenn, 13 over.

K: That Mom is going to be feeling better & the babies are going to come tomorrow nite at 5:30,

g: Happy about school.

52

BE GRATEFUL

Remember Oprah's idea of keeping a daily gratitude journal? Well, here it is with a tween twist.

Buy a blank notebook. Spend ten minutes at bedtime listing the top five things you are thankful for that day. Spend two minutes at breakfast. Make time to list a few at dinnertime. Just build it into some small part of your day. It's important.

Listen to your tween's entries.

Be prepared for anything: A flat-out "Nothing" might be the answer some days—for both of you! Other days there might be twelve entries and you have to make him choose his top five.

Talk about how different we can feel from one day to the next.

Spend a rainy morning decorating your grateful journal as a wonderful way to celebrate your lives together. Or spend a winter evening reading last year's entries, laughing or crying.

You won't ever feel like you wasted your time.

I beg my Mom to take me and my friends bowling. It's something I'm way better at than her!

Jess, 12

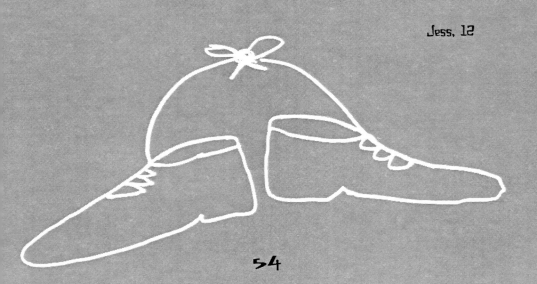

54

STRIKE OR SPARE?

Get that competitive tween off the couch and head for the bowling alley. Get a few of his friends to go with you and start a tween bowling team—one he can look forward to every week.

Book a Friday night slot at your local bowling alley and make it a standing date.

No one can help but laugh when you put on bowling shoes and hope you don't get another gutter ball.

There's no room for wimps here: No gutter bumpers allowed. The agony of defeat will get your tween's heart racing, and he'll start asking to go bowling just to practice.

Make sure the sodas and nachos are in good supply, and the spare change can be used for the pinball machine in the lobby.

Win or lose, no one strikes out when you're laughing together.

The videos of our plays are crazy. We've watched them over and over and still laugh!

Garrett, 10

HAM IT UP!

Act out a story from a book.

Our favorite at Halloween is *The Little Old Lady Who Wasn't Afraid of Anything* by Linda Williams. At holiday time, you might like to try *Something From Nothing* by Phoebe Gilman.

You can make these stories come alive with simple items you already have at home: shirt, shoes, hat and tie. Or try your neighborhood thrift stores for more costume and prop ideas.

Then have someone narrate the book as you act it out. Give everyone a part. Some might want to be stagehands while others want to ham it up.

Videotape the actors as a keepsake. Take it out when things are tough between you and your tween; you'll remember how much fun you two can have together. (Don't laugh too hard—your tween might think you're fun!)

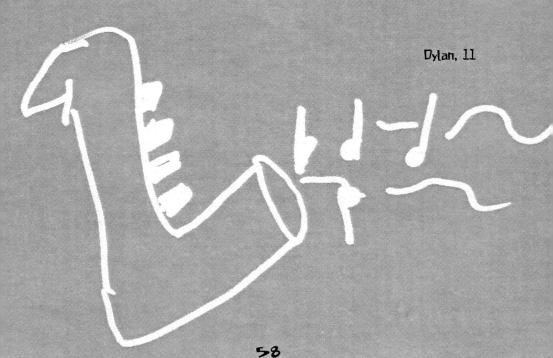

My advice here is to do it without the girls.

Dylan, 11

JAM SESSION 101

Go out on a limb and be the host house for your tween's first band. Have your middle-schooler pick a few friends—a mix of boys and girls who can sing, write songs or play an instrument.

Invite them over to your house and help them get organized. Help them pick a leader and get going with some lyrics they have in mind. The girls always seem to have the outfits and lyrics in place before the first jam session. Try to mix the lyrics with the kids' musical talent. It may not be easy on the ears, but it will be interesting to watch real negotiation in motion.

If you're not keen on loud music, grin and bear it. Be prepared for squabbles and take the time to put out a few fires among the young musicians. All creative types argue about who's in charge.

Make sure there's plenty of pop and chips and lend an ear when they write their first song.

Remember, you just might be hosting the next 'N Sync.

Collecting stuff always gives you something to do.

Kiefer, 8

WHAT'S IT WORTH?

Celebrate a common interest. Start a personal collection of something that's exciting to your tween. Make it something you both can get jazzed about.

Capture insects in your backyard. Go for a hike and search for geodes in the quarry. Research cool stamps. Start a pin-trading collection. Fill an autograph book with signatures of sports or music heroes. Build a trading card collection and visit card stores to pore over the cards you'd love to have.

Talk about great finds. And the "one that got away." Read trade publications that showcase the cool stuff your tween likes to collect.

Be sure to talk it up at social gatherings with your friends and theirs so your tween knows the interest is authentic—and you are too.

61

Sometimes my adopted grandparents cry when we come to sing. That's when I know we're helping them.

Kiefer, 8

Do Ya Care?

Don't sign your tween up for a trendy art camp. Pass on the soccer clinic this summer. Instead, host a camp that shows kids how to care about their community. Call it "Camp Care." It's easy.

Plan a weekly activity for a group of tweens who want to help in their neighborhood but don't know where to begin. That way, you'll make your house the cool place to be. Start first with a small group of your tween's friends. Brainstorm ideas about serving their community. Whatever the cause, you can help the kids make it work.

If music is their gig, help them to choose songs and rehearse instruments or sing along with a record. If they want to try their hand at Shakespeare, start thinking about costumes. Our school district offers costumes free to those who want to explore theater. Call around to see what your city has to offer or just use what you have in your closet.

Now you need to get the kids over often enough to learn their lines. Make it a fun Friday "tween" night in the summer. When you're all ready to take your show on the road, call local daycare centers or nursing homes to schedule a performance. It doesn't matter if you're good or not, the audience just loves the company.

And these are just a few ideas. Your won't live long enough to do all that your tween has in mind.

I wore my patched jeans to school, and everyone asked me, 'Camille, did you get those at the sample sale?' 'No, my mom and I made them!'

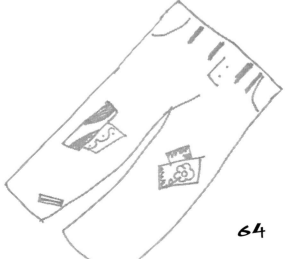

Camille, 10

SEW WHAT?

Knock off that designer wear and make it your own without paying beaucoup bucks!

Visit local boutiques and sample sales to get the basic ideas of what's "in" this season. Have your tween pick the styles she wants to copy and then head for a discount fabric store. Find the perfect end-bolts for $1.98 a yard and dig out the sewing machine.

We're no seamstresses, but we created some cool patches for a pair of used jeans for under $5! If you're no good at sewing, don't sweat it. No one is going to notice if the stitches on your knees aren't straight.

Instead of buying fabric, you can just pull some well-loved clothes out of storage. Cut them up and stitch a square of memories on the knees of an old pair of pants, the sleeve of a favorite sweater or right on a back pocket of your tween's jeans!

Then lie on her bed and reminisce about each swatch. Try not to cry. Your baby's growing up.

This one sounds kinda boring, but when you get started and someone likes your idea, you really get pumped!

Garrett, 10

LET FREEDOM RING

Find a topic your tween cares about. Sit down together and write an outline for an editorial essay.

Maybe it's about world peace, a community project she has started or just about the harried life of a tween. Let her know that she has a voice, and she deserves to be heard.

Help her organize her ideas in essay form and submit the essay to the local paper; be sure to include information about her age and school.

Chances are, if she has something to say, they'll print it. And chances are, if they print it, your tween will have caught the bug of journalism—or activism—at a young age.

If you're ever out West, we can tell you the best places to ski.

Dylan, 11

FIND THE BEST OF EVERYTHING

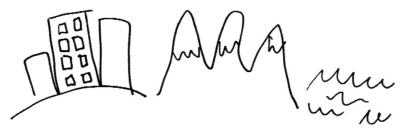

Rediscover your city. Find the best hot dogs, the best cheese pizza or the best place to watch the planes land. Have fun making up categories of your own.

These are not adult hot spots. Oh no. These spots are the best of the bests—in your tween's opinion.

Take a walk on the beach to discover the most secluded part of the surf; pedal your legs off to track down the best single-track mountain biking trail this side of the Mississippi, or spend a roll of quarters to choose the best game in the arcade. You'll have a blast finding the best deep powder in the back bowls or the perfect spot to snorkel or scuba dive off a sailboat to see the best underwater sights. You might even find that you've missed a lot of great stuff right where you live.

As your tween might say, "Whatever."

Go. Fight. Win!

Start a club. Maybe it's a running club, maybe it's a chess club, maybe it's a competition to get into the *Guinness World Records* book, or maybe it's just something you're tween is really good at.

Whatever it is, clear your idea with your school's extracurricular adviser. Book the field or classroom where you can "do your thing."

Your favorite tween can make posters or write an ad for the school newspaper to invite kids to join the fun. Draft a letter for parents to sign so their kid can learn something new.

Be the family that "started it all" at your school.

Oh, and you're the coach!

I like to sit on my Mom's bed,

listen to music and talk.

Jess,12

oM

Try some new relaxation tips to help your tween cope. There's lots happening in her life. Here are some techniques to help her cool out.

Spend time talking. Together. It might be at bedtime or it might be a moment in the morning; just make yourself available for what we call "Tween Talk": an open-ended conversation about "whatever."

Buy a blank journal for your tween. Encourage him to write or sketch in the book during stressful times. Or you can open your tween up to the healing powers of prayer with the gift of a pocket-size Bible. Or let music soothe the stress away. Place a few calming CDs on your tween's shelf so she can reach up and try something new.

Add a soothing leg massage with lavendar oil to her bedtime ritual. Those growing legs and overworked calves will thank you. Talk about what it means to nurture your spiritual self.

You'll be surprised at how much he'll thank you.

When you go to the shelter, don't worry that the people will be scary; they're all nice and kind.

Kiefer, 8

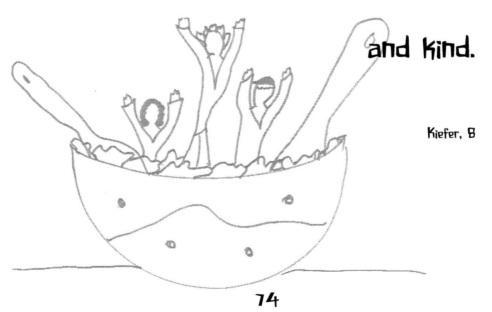

CHIEF COOK AND BOTTLE WASHER

Make dinner for a local homeless shelter and dine with the people staying there.

Get out the telephone directory. Take a quick look under "Homeless Shelters." Sadly, there will be plenty to choose from. Every shelter has needs. Contact the volunteer coordinator. Ask for the dinner schedule and sign up for an evening.

Spend an afternoon baking a truck-load of lasagna and fresh bread and fixing a big tossed salad. Put your tween in charge of dessert, and the cookies or brownies will be gourmet quality.

Then head down to the shelter with your piping hot dinner in tow. Be sure to take along a deck of cards, a stack of books and a musical instrument to entertain the crowd after dinner.

Go home feeling full in more ways than one.

Anytime there's a cake on
the table, I'm excited!

Jenn, 13

READY? SET. SURPRISE!

Plan a surprise party for the rest of the family. Do it when no one is expecting a celebration.

It's not for a birthday. It's not for a job well done. It's just "Because."

Make it BIG. Bake a cake and make your family's favorite foods. Eat in the dining room, and use your best dishes. Light candles. Have balloons at every place.

Make place cards with each person's picture. Use cloth napkins and fancy rings. Watch home movies or the birth of each child on video. Or surprise one kid for a job well-done. Or a season of heart.

Pop popcorn and laugh about how it feels to be surprised out of your shoes.

No presents, please. Sharing your laughter and memories is the gift you give each other.

Make every wall a different color.

Then it feels like you're moving

into a new place.

Camille, 10

FENG SHUI, A TWEEN'S WAY

Borrow a book on Feng Shui from your library. Find out all you can about the ancient art of understanding the energy—or ch'i—that surrounds us. Then pick a room and decorate it the feng shui way. It might be your tween's favorite reading nook or his bedroom. It might be her bathroom.

Agree on the cost, limiting it to $20, $50 or $100. And then let it rip. Learn that the color green speaks to new beginnings, and blue radiates knowledge. Pick your tween's brain by listening to her color choices. It might bring the conversation around to bigger and meatier subjects.

Then plan where all his stuff goes. And what new doodad he just *has* to have. Hit a few garage sales, Grandma's attic or secondhand stores to find the perfect overstuffed chair. Pore over paint chips and fabric swatches to pick the brightest cranberry in the bunch. Give all the sports paraphernalia a place of honor.

Remember that the journey is 90 percent of the fun here, and when it's all said and done, you might be secretly sad. So pick another room and do it all over again.

I really like our Book Club, and I hope to stay with it till we're adults.

Alexis, 10

BE BOOKWORMS TOGETHER

Start a Parent/Tween Book Club. Shireen Dodson, author of *The Mother-Daughter Book Club,* sets the stage for a wonderful experience between moms and their daughters.

Pick a book you love and want to share with about seven parent/tween pairs. Send out the invitations and provide a sign-up sheet for the whole year so everyone gets a chance to host at least once a year.

Our club meets once a month (we've been going strong for three years now), and we find that talking about literature is a great way to find out a lot about who our tweens are. We've enjoyed more than one inspirational book discussion led by our tweens and have welcomed authors, tasted new cuisine and shared journal entries.

Sometimes you can do some cooking to tell the story. Or maybe you can meet at an unusual location to make the book come alive. Either way, your tween will look forward to a good read—and an adventure.

We guarantee it!

A good football game

can happen in

about ten minutes.

Then, watch out!

Dylan, 11

FOURTH DOWN. A YARD TO GO.

*G*et your old cleats down from the closet shelf and dust them off. Pick a beautiful fall day when the leaves have turned golden and fallen to the ground. Then get out your tween's address book and start calling.

You're looking to build your own winning football team. It won't take too long to find a few more father/tween pairs who are looking for a way out of raking those leaves. Go to your local park and mix it up, fair and square.

Make sure there's plenty of Gatorade on ice. Laugh about the times you counted "one, two, three Mississippi" faster than you ever thought possible. (Remember the rule book?)

Take a snapshot of the teams' winning smiles.

Dinner tastes better when

the stuff is from your garden.

Garrett, 10

4 GREEN THUMBS ARE BETTER THAN 2

Plant an herb garden—or a full-blown vegetable/flower garden—and tend it together. Weed it. Water it. Care for it to make it thrive.

Get dirt under your fingernails and mud on the soles of your clogs and laugh about the joys of gardening. Plant tomatoes, flowers and lettuce to harvest a healthy crop.

Plan meals that call for the herbs from your garden. Or throw a "Grow Your Own Dinner" party for your tween's friends and make a pomodoro pasta dish using basil from his very own garden. Toss a fresh arugula salad with cherry tomatoes and chives from your backyard. Dress up your table with fresh flowers from your garden.

Sit back and smile.

The food at our potluck isn't always the stuff I like, but we do have fun.

Dylan, 11,

Bon Appetit!

Here's a fun twist on an old idea. It's called "Potluck with a Purpose," and it's fun for all ages. It's a night of potluck fun—with a cultural theme—where everyone gets in on the cooking and the learning.

Call up a few tween/adult pairs who would love an excuse to try a new dish and enjoy a different ethnic cuisine every month. Then pick a region and start to cook something authentic. One month we laughed our pants off as we made authentic dolmades (that's stuffed grape leaves, to me and you). Another time we had lots of fun pressing, cooking and eating our own tortillas with all the trimmings.

Remember to share a folk tale or favorite book from the featured region. We read *Too Many Tamales* by Gary Soto as we pigged-out on chips and salsa. We can't guarantee that your tween will like the fare as much as he likes burgers and fries, but, hey, he's trying something new with you.

Bon Appetit!

My Mom always says,

'Everybody's an artist.'

Camille, 10

CALLING ALL ARTISTS

Host a neighborhood art gallery. Go door-to-door and find every budding artist who has work to show off.

Collect all the artwork and contact local framing companies—the bigger the better—that might donate used mat boards. Mat all the works of art and ask neighbors to loan every card table that isn't being used for the Friday night poker game. If you want a simpler framing option, try some recycled frames, available for next to nothing at a thrift shop.

Display the works of art in your own backyard. You can staple it to trees, hang it on clotheslines or prop it up against the fence.

Make some attractive posters to advertise your big art gallery show and sale. Then let art lovers of all ages come by to see the work of the neighborhood's masters. Admission is $1, and you can even buy your kid's pieces back to save for posterity. All proceeds go to a local charity.

Who wouldn't want to be famous for a day?

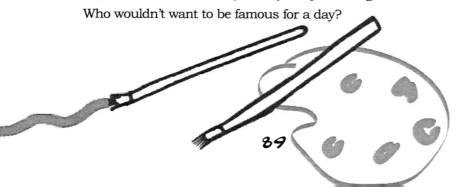

Mom always says the water slide is too dangerous. Until she wants to cool off!

Garrett, 10

SOME LIKE IT HOT!

Kids like it hot.

So enjoy a scorching summer day with your tween, doing just what they like to do to cool down: Play.

Get out in the backyard and laugh your way through his makeshift water obstacle course. He's rigged the hose on the slide to make it slick, and the dunk tank—made from your plastic kiddie pool—is perfectly positioned at the base of the slide. You *will* get wet. And the two of you will laugh.

There's no escaping now. You're spending the day at Tween World—a theme park like no other. And if it seems as if the water balloons always end up bursting in your face, it's no coincidence.

You're on your tween's turf!

Making brownies for the neighbors is great because I get to lick the bowl!

Jess, 12

BUTCHER, BAKER, CANDLESTICK MAKER

Mark the first Sunday of every month and be a butcher, baker or candlestick maker for your neighbors.

Make candles, bake mini loaves of seven-grain bread or share some of the fall hunt or summer catch. Welcome the new neighbors with some freshly baked brownies and a warm hello. Make your favorite chocolate chip cookie recipe for an elderly neighbor, just 'cuz.

Wrap the bounty in warm tea towels and a big, red bow. Attach a homemade note that reads, "You're Just Terrific." Stop by for a chat or just ring and run! It's fun to be nice.

And it's sure to brighten someone else's day—and yours.

There's nothing like being with my Dad.

Ginny Cumber, 12 [1949]

Ginny's Mom, Ginny Cumber, gives her Dad, Lee, a hug.

JUST THE TWO OF US

Find a special place that has significance for the two of you and visit it at least twice a year.

Make it a place that says something about your relationship with your tween. Think of it as a part of your history together.

Maybe it's the weeping willow tree on Grandpa's farm or the swings that you played on when you were young or a trip to an old-fashioned ice cream parlor for a sundae with marshmallow-cream topping.

Visit your special place in two different seasons and talk about how it makes you feel. Get out your grateful journals and document your feelings that day.

Or tell the story in watercolors.

Just the two of you.

Nothing relaxes me like music.

Jenn, 13

Box Your Stress Away!

We call it the De-Stress Yourself Box, and it has helped put out the fire when words can't. Fill a simple basket or box with things that can help your tween do some self-soothing of her own. Come on. Start thinking.

What might go inside?

Maybe you could throw a funny, knock-knock joke book in for a few belly laughs.

Maybe you can add a copy of the New Testament in the box and open your tween's heart up to prayer. Or maybe there's something really special—such as his favorite music or book on tape with a set of headphones—that only your tween would enjoy.

Pick a few really wacky photos of your tween doing some pretty silly stuff and throw them in for good measure. Now put it in a quiet room of the house and make it easy to use.

Try to walk in your tween's shoes and remember, it's a lot harder than when we were there.

Picks from our Jar!

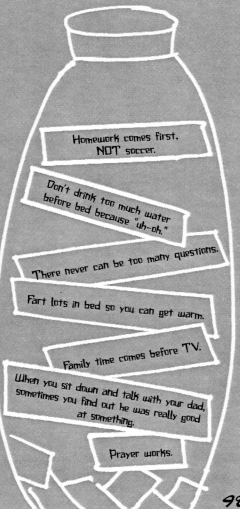

HERE'S WHAT I DO KNOW

Every tween feels that adults spend their days teaching them what they need to know.

Try this: Create a "Here's What I *Do* Know" jar of inspiration. Give a big glass jar a place of prominence in the kitchen and have paper and pen handy. Encourage your tween to write down new phrases, definitions of new words, new concepts or life experiences. Toss them into the jar.

Maybe it's as simple as, "Never leave long-term projects till the last day."

Sounds easy? We don't think so. How long did it take you to get life's little lessons all figured out?

Chances are, your tween won't be the only one using this jar.

Working out with your Dad tells you he wants you to be good at something.

Jenn, 13

PUMP IT UP!

Start a new fitness regime with your tween. Visit your health club and lift weights, pedal the stationary bike, shoot some hoops. Or go all-out and train for a triathlon together.

You can develop your new fitness regime with him in mind.

If he likes to cycle, visit an indoor track and see the pros at work. Go to a local university and watch a wrestling match or basketball final.

Inspire yourself and your tween and make it a full-body commitment packed with protein shakes and leg waxings. Or just scale it down and eat right and get your heart rate up three times a week.

Do whatever makes your time together something to remember.

Make it a contest where you're both the winners.

YOU BE BLACK, I'LL BE RED

Dust off the checkerboard and challenge your tween to a rousing game of checkers. Better yet, learn how to play chess again with your tween as your chess coach.

Challenge yourself to one of those difficult LEGO® creations with the master at your side. Try your hand at a 1,500-piece puzzle or take a stab at building with some cool building blocks. Or just grab a ball and play a game of 2-square.

Don't play just one game. Commit to two hours of really playing a game with your tween.

How long has it been?

I still sleep with my teddy bear that I bought the day my Dad and I had our birthday party together. I won't ever forget it.

Kiefer, 8

HAPPY BIRTHDAY TO US

Pick a random date to celebrate your relationship with your tween. Make sure it's a long way from his real birthday and even farther away from the big, gift-giving holidays.

Look forward to it. Talk about what would be fun for both of you.

Take a hike. Or just stay in your pj's all day and refinish an old desk. Go for a sail. Go fishing. Paint by the beach. Take an elderly friend out for lunch. Plan your fantasy vacation—on paper.

Do whatever you and your tween love to do.

Then buy a cake. Put candles on it for every year you've known each other. Make a wish and blow them out. Give each other a hug.

Make it an annual event not to be missed!

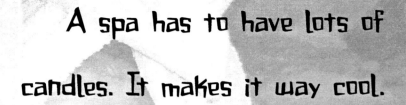

MASSAGE, ANYONE?

Go to a spa in your own home. Yup, that's right. Transform your bathroom into your tween's spa for a night. Set the mood with lighted candles and a bubbly bath. Have her warmest bathrobe and toasty slippers laid out as she soaks her hands in a lavender paraffin wax dip. And then she'll want to do her feet.

Next, treat her to a bubble bath surrounded by lighted candles and the sounds of the ocean in the background. After a soak in the tub, have the spa staff escort her to a night of finger and toenail painting, peppermint foot rubs and cucumber eye treatments—simple luxuries you'll find in any five and dime store.

When she's thoroughly relaxed, she can retire to the kitchen to make her own personal lotions and soaps before she curls up in bed for a reading from Maureen Garth's meditation book, *Earthlight*.

You might be surprised to find that pampering your tween makes you feel good too. . . . Ahh!

I can't wait to put my signature on the mural.

Jess, 12

Be Vincent Van Gogh!

Leave your mark on the world. Paint a mural on the side of a barn that could use a pick-me-up or a city building that needs a new look.

Have some rough sketches of your ideas on paper. Contact local paint stores for free supplies. Get a lot. Then gather a team from your school, church youth group or just a bunch of neighbors interested in working together to make America even more beautiful.

Then you're ready for the pitch. Visit farms with a knock on the door and a smile on your face or tell the city property owner your ideas for free art for his building. Then plan which Sundays your team of artists will be there and follow through.

You might end up with some paint on your face, but we can assure you, you won't be blue.

SHARE YOUR FAVORITE BOOKS

Maybe you need a good reason to snuggle up next to your tween and read a picture book. Well, here's ours.

It's a literacy program for homeless kids that we call "Almost Home Bookshelf." We've been reading to the kids at the shelter since 1997. It's a no-brainer because it doesn't cost anything but your time.

Look in the phone book and pick a homeless shelter in your area. Talk to the volunteer coordinator and offer to start a literacy program. Have your tween tap friends and family as well as local schools and churches to donate their gently used books. In no time, you'll have a full-blown library.

Make sure your tween inspects the mountain of books you'll receive and then helps you truck them down to the shelter. Let your tween organize the books where they can be readily available to small hands.

Then, one Sunday evening a month, arrive at the shelter right after dinner and read for an hour. Encourage your tween to get down on the floor with the little ones and read *Goodnight Moon* ten times. Remind him how many times you read that classic to him. Encourage the kids to love reading books by letting them pick their favorites to take to their next home.

Nurture your library. Keep the donations coming. Take stock of what you and your tween have together.

Make sure you're there one Sunday night a month. Sit back and feel proud that some at-risk kids might learn to love to read by reading with you and your tween.

Going to the homeless shelter makes me feel like I have so much.

Camille, 10

TWINKLE, TWINKLE, MY LITTLE STAR

Make a wish. And put it in a box. A very special wish box.

Make a wish box every year on New Year's Eve. Grab any box you might have in the corner of the basement. Write down one important wish for yourself, one for your family and one for the world on a sheet of paper.

Don't hope for an end to world hunger. Everyone wants to win the lottery. Instead, make a wish that you can make happen through hard work. Identify ways that you could make your wish come true. Maybe it's a no-bullying pact with someone at school or an offer to brighten an elderly person's day once a month. These are things we all can do.

Put your wishes in the box. Then get some brightly colored wrapping paper, ribbon and tape and wrap it. Make it look like there's something very special inside. Then pick a place of importance for your box of hope—the mantelpiece over your fireplace or the top shelf of your family library—and open it on the following New Year's Day.

See what wishes you made come true!

I always want my Mom to say

goodnight to me longer.

Dylan, 11

SO NOW WHAT?

You say you've come to the end of the book, and you've tried all 52 journeys—and you want more?

Well, while you're waiting for Volume Two of *Tween Time*, don't waste time. Do the easiest and cheapest thing you can do with your tween: Say goodnight.

That's right. Go up to her room. Don't just pat her head in the living room. Go and rub her back. Kiss her forehead. Ask about his day. Read aloud. Give him a big bear hug.

Say goodnight. Every night.

THE BIG THANKS

No joke. We didn't write this book alone. *Tween Time* is in print because so many people believed in us.

To Jim and Mary Cohen, for their generous support. They made us remember your best friends are the ones you met in kindergarten.

To Bunky Kampic for her generous support. It goes to show you, you never know who you might meet at the laundromat.

To Dorota Bednarczyk. Now we both helped each other make it.

To Ginny and Brett Kaehn, for saving for *our* rainy day.

To Michelle Munroe for putting the big splash on our Web site, www.TweenTime.com.

To Maureen Cotter, who dotted our "i's" and crossed our "t's."

To the whole Scobie Family for making their support a family affair.

To Christine Testolini, for all her professional advice. She proved that there is great karma at every cocktail party.

To Lori Frank, who taught us that sixth-grade English teachers are pretty smart.

To Julie DeRoin and Bryan McGrath, who started the ball rolling.

To Sue Lubeck, who believes in all those who dream big.

And to all the hundred that gave a hundred! You're the best!

GiNNY BiSHoP is a mother of six children who loves spending time with kids, big or small. She calculates that by the time she hits 50, she will have celebrated 24 years of raising tweens (including twin tweens—the babies of the family.) She lives with her husband, Joe, and their kids in Littleton, Colorado, and has never stopped wishing on stars. Ginny earned a master's degree in Corporate Communications from Northwestern University.

KIM GRIFFETH has never minded getting her hands messy in a big way. She earned her bachelor's degree at the University of Colorado and works as a director of a Learning-Through-Play preschool program and spends her nights looking for the Big Dipper. Kim—a single mother of three—also lives in Littleton and still believes in Santa Claus.

CAMiLLE SOLARTE is a 10-year-old artist who dreams big! She wants to be a famous illustrator one day; *Tween Time* is her first shot. She draws almost every minute she is awake. The rest of her time is spent in fifth grade at St. Anne's Episcopal School and at soccer practice. She is one of Ginny and Joe's six children, and she dreams of being an only child in her next life.

GREG MONTEZON is the founder of Montezon Design and is a designer who likes challenges. From designs on paper to items you can hold, his designs always have a playful twist to them. He lives in Chicago with his wife, Michelle, who inspires him every day. He gets lots of "tween time" visiting with his seventeen nieces and nephews. Greg has a Design/Industrial Design Degree from the Milwaukee Institute of Art and Design.

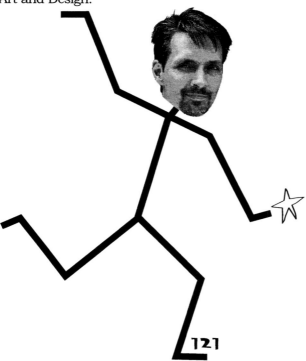

OR GO TO
WWW.TWEENTIME.COM
AND ORDER YOUR COPY ONLINE!

We want to hear from you!
You can reach us on the web at:

www.tweentime.com

Let's Share Tween Stories.

Visit us on the Web at **WWW.TWEENTIME.COM** and tell us about the fun things you do with the tween in your life. We'd love to hear from you!

If you want to order *Tween Time* online, you're just a click away at **WWW.TWEENTIME.COM.** Or visit our Web site to schedule a *Tween Time* workshop in your area.

We're here to help you get out of your routine and into spending time with that terrific tween in your life.

WE WOULD LOVE TO HEAR YOUR STORY.

YOU CAN REACH US AT:

WWW.TWEENTIME.COM

LET'S HAVE COFFEE

We have a *Tween Time* workshop that will inspire everyone in your audience to try one of our magical journeys today!

So invite us over to your next PTA meeting, church get-together, annual home-schooling conference or Mother/Daughter Book Club session and let us share with your audience some new and fun ideas on staying connected with that special tween in their lives.

It's easy.

Just contact us at **WWW.TWEENTIME.COM**, and we'll be happy to tailor our workshop to your needs.

We'd love to hear from you!

WATCH FOR OTHER BOOKS AND PRODUCTS FROM:

Happy Life Press
P.O. Box 270556
Littleton, CO 80127
HappyLifePress@aol.com